I0372764

A Hare's Tale 3
The Pharoahs

Rob Auty

Illustrations by
Chaz Wood
www.chaz-wood.com

2QT Limited (Publishing)

First Edition published 2014 by
2QT Limited (Publishing)
www.2qt.co.uk

Copyright © Robert C Auty

The right of Robert C Auty to be identified as the author
of this work has been asserted by him in accordance with the
Copyright, Designs and Patents Act 1988

All rights reserved. This book is sold subject to the condition that no part of this book is to be reproduced, in any shape or form. Or by way of trade, stored in a retrieval system or transmitted in any form or by any means, electronic, mechanical, photocopying, recording, be lent, re-sold, hired out or otherwise circulated in any form of binding or cover other than that in which it is published and without a similar condition, including this condition being imposed on the subsequent purchaser, without prior permission of the copyright holder.

Illustrations by Chaz Wood
Cover by Tim Budgen
Typesetting by Dale Rennard

Printed in Great Britain
Lightning Source UK Ltd

A CIP catalogue record for this book is available
from the British Library
ISBN 978-1-910077-07-8

Authors Note : Special thanks to all the contributors, particularly Chaz, Tim, and Dale. And to Sharon Wilding for all her input and support during the creation of the 'A Hare's Tale' series.

Thank you all.

Contents

Prologue

Chapter One - The Hunters 9

Chapter Two - The Animals 15

Chapter Three - Colin Sweevil 21

Chapter Four - Yar Turps........................... 35

Chapter Five - Lord Snoot 43

Chapter Six - Liam, and the Pharoahs............ 57

Chapter Seven - Help from the Darkness 77

Chapter Eight - Yar Turps and Samantha 81

Chapter Nine - Tim the 'Vet-n-ary' 85

Chapter Ten - Farmer 93

Chapter Eleven - The Animals, and

One Giant Rat 97

Hare Epilogue....................................... 105

A Hunter's Epilogue 108

Epilogue... 110

The Pharoahs   Rob Auty

Prologue

Patrick lay flat on the big sofa. He sighed heavily and looked again at the contents of the coffee table in front of him. Something he saw there made him sit up and grab a half-concealed magazine from beneath a pile of newspapers. An article about the hunting of Hares had caught his attention. He read the article, and as he did his eyes widened. 'Mum!' he shouted in alarm.

Samantha rushed in the room expecting the worse; such was the dread in Patrick's voice. 'What's wrong, Darling?' she asked her son.

'Look at this! Is this right? How can they do that!' He thrust the magazine towards her.

Samantha knew what he was referring to. She had read the article herself only a couple of hours earlier. 'Sadly, yes,' she told him, 'some people, it seems, do not consider their consciences or...' and Samantha paused, considering her words carefully, '...the consequences of their actions.'

'I don't know what that means,' Patrick said angrily. 'They're killing Hares for fun, for sport!' he added indignantly.

'It means, that many hunters do not consider tomorrow, and the fact that if they continue to kill for *sport* as they do, there won't be any Hares left for *sport* in a few years time, or any other animals come to that,' Samantha told him.

'It's not right!' Patrick said; he looked upset.

'Many things aren't, Darling,' Samantha said, 'but I can tell you a story about Juney if you want, where hunters don't always win.'

'Another Hare's Tale?' Patrick asked excitedly.

'Yes!'

A few minutes later found them cuddled on the couch.

Prologue

'Are we…' Samantha started.

'Sitting comfortably! Yes!' Patrick finished.

'Then I'll begin…'

The Cherrywood Hare

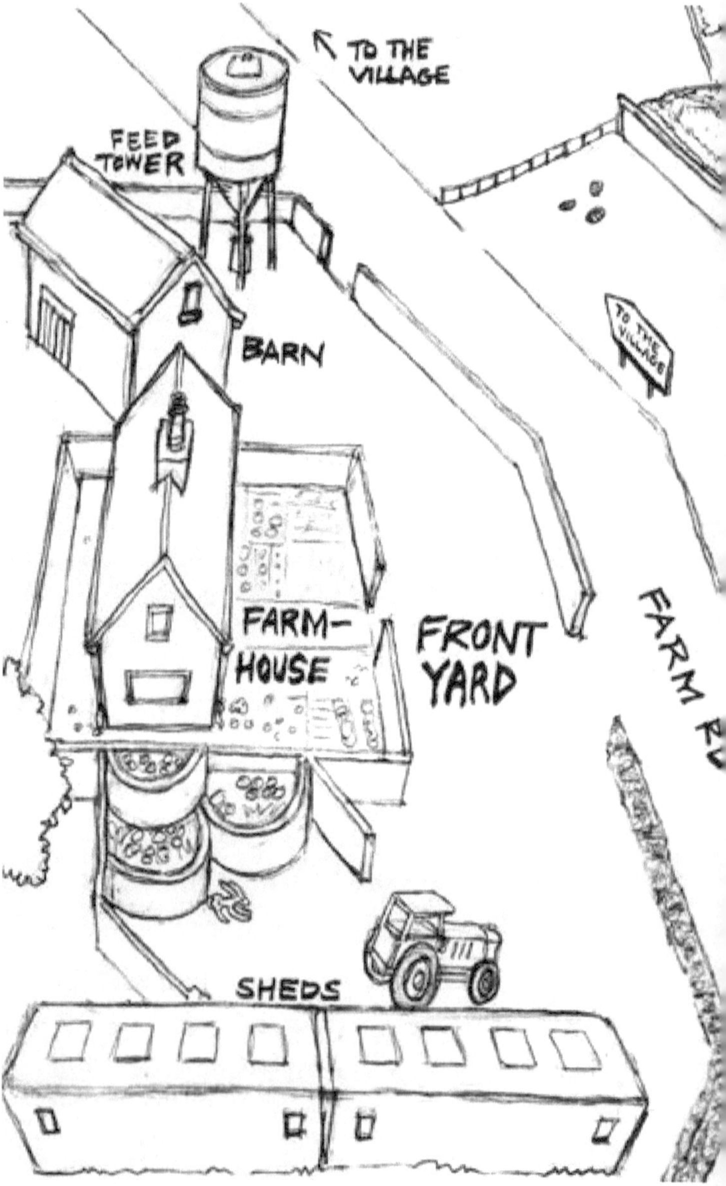
TO THE VILLAGE
FEED TOWER
BARN
TO THE VILLAGE
FARM-HOUSE
FRONT YARD
FARM RD
SHEDS

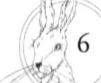

Prologue

The Pharoahs   Rob Auty

Chapter One
The Hunters

'There she is,' Bograt peered through the binoculars at the distant meadow.

Bograt

He stood on a hill, and he was not alone. It was a warm, sunny day, and the sky was clear.

'Let me look,' Lord Snoot grabbed the binoculars and eagerly put them to his small, beady eyes. 'Ah, yes! My goodness, she is golden, that pelt will be worth a fortune, or even better, stuffed and mounted on my mantelpiece! My Beagles and Harriers will enjoy the chase!'

'That Jack with her has to be the biggest Hare I've ever seen!' Yar Turps, the tinker, stared towards the field at the large Jack, with the odd tuft of hair between his massive ears. He didn't seem to need the field glasses. 'Must be at least fifteen pounds, and she don't look much less. They's gonna be difficult prey.'

'Let me see,' Colin Sweevil said. He was a strange character and held out a skinny hand to Lord Snoot, who handed him the binoculars. 'She looks fast, and I've never seen Hares acting like that, there must be more than twenty of them in

Chapter One *The Hunters*

that field and it's late summer, they don't usually gather like that.' He wore a greatcoat, well past his knees, and the collar turned up around his weasel-like face.

'You really offering a thousand pounds?' a tall man asked. He was standing behind the other men. He had a wide handsome face and a wild shock of red hair. He wore a tight leather coat, carried a shotgun over the crook of his left arm, and had two odd looking dogs sat either side of him. They were short coated, almost orange in colour, and had keen wedge shaped faces, with sharp, alert ears.

Cleo and Rameses

'I am, Liam. She's caused me no end of grief, and a hefty fine from the police to boot,' Bograt declared.

'Well we can't all go blundering after her; Lurchers, Beagles, Harriers, and my Hounds, and not to mention your Hawks, Colin. We need a plan, or maybe we should have a competition, with Bograt's thousand as a prize?' Liam offered, with a sly smile.

'I want that Hare, and I want that golden coat!' Lord Snoot declared. 'And I'm prepared to pay well.'

'Really? Well now that sounds very interesting,' Liam said.

'Should we draw straws to decide who gets first try?' Colin suggested.

'Not a bad idea,' Liam said.

So Bograt arranged some small twigs into three long, and one short length, and then he let the men pick. He repeated the draw three times until an order had emerged. Colin Sweevil would

Chapter One   *The Hunters*

hunt with his Hawks on the first day, tomorrow, Friday. Then Yar Turps would *Lamp* the Hares on that night, should Colin fail. Lord Snoot would hunt with his Hounds on the Saturday, and then, if the Golden Hare was still free, Liam would hunt on the Saturday night.

Liam looked quite angry, and Colin's smile threatened to split his thin face in half. 'That'll be my thousand pounds then,' he gloated.

'Don't be so sure, none of ye, that there is a special creature. From what Bograt ha told us, she'll run us all ragged and be a hard hunt,' Yar Turps told them.

'No guns,' Colin stated firmly.

'No guns,' they all agreed, Liam rather grudgingly.

'I'll give an extra thousand to anyone for the pelt, or the Hare intact, if you take her before me,' Lord Snoot declared.

'Now just a minute,' Bograt stated indignantly, 'this is my competition and I get the Hare!'

'I wouldn't worry too much, Bograt, if Snoot's Beagles get her, there won't be anything left for anyone. On the other hand, if Cleopatra, and Rameses here get a chance, along with their brothers and sisters,' Liam indicated his prize hounds, 'then I can promise a near whole Hare, and then we can discuss a price…'

'Only a thousand!' Bograt squealed.

'We'll see, we'll see,' Liam smirked.

None of the men noticed the Magpie alighting on the telephone line above them.

Chapter Two
The Animals

'Juney! Juney!' Mollie the Magpie landed heavily amongst the startled Hares, many of them darted away, looking for cover, leaving only three, Juney, Tufty Thomas, and Slow Freddy.

'What's wrong, Mollie?' Juney asked quietly, she was used to Mollie's sudden appearances. She absently combed one of her long ears with a front foot.

'Men are coming for you! Men with Hawks, Hounds, and strange dogs I've never seen before!'

'Why, Mollie?' Freddy asked.

'Bograt's got them fired up; offering *a thousand pounds*, whatever that is, and they look a mean bunch. They want Juney, and they want her golden coat!'

'We should all run, and leave them with no Hares at all! We can all go to Four Fields, we've friends there now, and Juney will be welcome any place we go, all the animals know the Golden Hare is with us now,' Tufty Thomas suggested.

Tufty

Chapter Two   *The Animals*

Juney thought for a moment, her nose twitched, and she tapped one of her big back feet on the ground. 'And wherever the Golden Hare goes, trouble will follow, ' she said finally. 'I will stay, and, I will defeat these men and their creatures. I must, if I run, they, or others, will follow and Hares will be forever in danger. No! I will stay and I will beat them in the hunt!'

Other Hares had slowly ventured from hiding places, and three were far ahead of the others; Juney's Leverets, Big Toe Timmy, Short Eared Sal, and Feisty Frank. 'We'll all stay too!' Frank declared.

'Hares are always in danger anyway,' Marty Lop Ear declared. 'Let them come,' he added fiercely. A Hare acting fiercely doesn't really work, and the others laughed, but you wouldn't have known it. Only a Hare knows when another Hare is laughing.

'No!' Freddy shouted, 'Juney is right; the only way for us to be safe is if Juney becomes ... *Legend*

… amongst the humans. If she defeats them all in the hunt, then few will attempt to hunt her again.'

'My Leverets will go with the Hares to Four Fields,' Juney stated. Frank and his brother protested noisily and Thomas gave them both a stern look, quieting them. Sal sidled up to her mother's side and began to groom the Golden Hare.

Surprisingly, Freddy took charge and ordered the Hares away, until only he, Thomas, and Mollie remained with Juney.

'Mollie go, see and listen to what is going on, find out what the men are up to,' Freddy said authoritatively.

Mollie saluted him cheekily with her wing, and then flew off.

'You're being very strong, Freddy,' Juney said happily. She had always been Freddy's best friend.

'I wear Wimble's glasses, and I am the teacher now. I may be fat and slow, and scared, Juney, but I

am smart, and those men face more than the Golden Hare!' Freddy stood tall, his frame wobbling.

Neither Juney nor Thomas laughed, as they might once have.

The Pharoahs Rob Auty

Chapter Three
Colin Sweevil

Colin ambled down the slope with Bay, his Harris Hawk, quiet and hooded on his hand, and a small terrier at his heels. Yar Turps followed, a Goshawk sitting on his gloved hand. The bird appeared tense, probably as a result of Yar's outstretched arm, keeping the fearsome hawk as far away as possible. Liam followed with a very large Gyr Falcon on his arm. Liam was relaxed and happy, and it showed in the bird's demeanour. Lord Snoot and Bograt puffed and panted as they followed the younger and fitter men.

'That's an unusual collection of animals, Colin,' Lord Snoot said.

'I love my Hawks,' Colin replied, 'I brought Falco,' he nodded towards the bird Liam carried, 'because those Hares are big. I'll try Bay here first, see what she can do, and then Goose,' he indicated the bird Yar held, 'and if they aren't successful, Falco will fly and he's never failed me.' Colin looked adoringly at Falco.

'Well I've never seen anything like that before,' Liam said, pointing into the distance. The Golden Hare sat, admittedly some distance away, and calmly watched them.

'I tell you all, I is gettin' seriously worried

about this already,' Yar stated. 'There is sometin' not quite right with that animal, it ain't natural at all!'

'Stop mithering, Yar,' Liam said. 'If you don't want to hunt, withdraw, and let me take your place tonight.' Liam smiled nastily at the tinker.

'I'll hunt tonight, Liam, but you just mark my words!' Yar snapped back.

In the meantime Colin had taken the hood off Bay, the Harris Hawk, and he was whispering to the excited animal. Suddenly, without a word, he threw his hand skyward and Bay took off, screaming her excitement.

Juney sat still and watched the approach of the Hawk. The bird flew high, and seeing its stationary prey, it dived towards Juney at breathtaking speed. Juney waited, tensing her muscles, and just when it seemed the bird would strike she took off.

'Wow, she just missed! Up my beauty! Up Bay!' Colin shouted.

The bird took to the sky again and rose high to look for the Hare. Juney moved around, so the bird could see her again, and then she began to slowly run. The bird finally caught sight of her and moved excitedly, trying to create another striking opportunity. Juney ran into the long, tough grass on the side of the hill, and then popped her head up, waiting for the Hawk. It saw her there, and arrowed towards her. Once again, at the last minute, Juney disappeared and the bird struck the ground hard, and floundered in the long grass, it screamed its distress, and was obviously struggling to take off again.

'Stupid bird!' Colin squealed. He spent some minutes recalling Bay, feeding, hooding and securing her on Liam's other hand. Meanwhile the Hare had once again taken up her original position and stared back at the hunters.

'She's mocking you, Colin,' Liam smirked.

'Let her mock this then,' Colin screeched. He freed the bird from Yar's hand, and released it himself. 'Up Goose, up my girl!' he encouraged the Goshawk. Then he took Falco from Liam and released him as well. 'Fly Falco, bring me the Hare!'

'That's stupid, Colin, they'll interfere with each other,' Yar said.

'Watch and learn, I've been training them. Falco will wait and bide his time. If Goose is successful, he'll fly back to me,' Colin replied confidently.

Juney watched the new bird; it seemed more confident and assured than the first. She ran, very fast, zigzagging across the grass. And the bird followed. No matter where she ran the bird was ever present, just a few dozen feet above her. She could not stop, as in the first attack, because this Hawk stayed too close. It dived, and struck, fast and devilishly hard, taking a few golden hairs in its talon. But Juney was still free. The bird rose quickly and soon had her sighted again, and once again, Juney had to flee. She ran uphill and jigged and rolled, trying to throw her attacker off, but its keen eyes kept it within striking range, and it dived again.

'Goose has it!' Colin jumped in the air as he shouted.

'No! It's another Hare, the big Jack. He's made a mess of your bird, Colin,' Liam said, chuckling.

The men watched; the Goshawk had struck another Hare, with an odd mop of hair between its big ears, which had popped up out of a thicket of grass, between itself and the Golden Hare. The Hawk took the new Hare on the hip, and then the Hare squealed and rolled over and over, squashing the Hawk and leaving it stunned and damaged on the grassy slope.

'Blasted beasts! Falco, kill them!' Colin was hopping from one foot to another, gesticulating with his arms.

Chapter Three *Colin Sweevil*

Falco watched, as he had been trained to do, until his smaller cousin had failed, and then he moved with purpose. A great shadow above him drew his attention and, as he looked back, a mighty Eagle flew towards him at impossible speed and angle, knocking him out of his glide. Falco, without a backward look, flew away, returning to the safety of his human.

Aquila slowed her attack and let the Gyr Falcon flee. She flew towards the Hares and landed next to her injured friend, Tufty Thomas.

'Did you see that? Did you see that?' Yar Turps cried.

Liam shrugged, 'Yeah, you don't see Eagles very often,' he conceded.

Colin screeched unintelligible words as he kicked the terrier, 'Go, you stupid dog, do your job,' he yelled.

The terrier took off towards the Hares. The men watched as the terrier ran eagerly towards the prey. Liam laughed out loud as the Eagle ran at the dog, wings outstretched. The terrier, barked half-heartedly, and then ran away. Not back towards Colin, just away and he was out of sight within a few seconds.

Chapter Three   *Colin Sweevil*

'Thank you, Aquila,' Juney said.

'Is the bravest of Hares hurt?' Aquila asked.

'I'm fine, Aquila,' said Tufty Thomas, 'I'll be sore for a few days though.'

'You were stupid, I told you I'd handle things!' Juney admonished him.

'Sorry,' Thomas muttered.

'I saw, Juney, Thomas saved you. You are fast, the fastest I've ever seen, but that bird nearly had you, and Thomas was there at exactly the right time,' Aquila told her.

Juney appeared to want to stay angry, but then she rubbed her nose against Thomas' hip, where the talons had bitten, and said, 'Thank you, Tufty, and thank *you*, Aquila.'

The Goshawk was stirring, and it rose groggily from the ground. It appeared to have a damaged wing.

'We should go,' Thomas said, as he watched the men approach.

'Good luck, Golden Hare,' Aquila cried as she rose quickly into the air.

Tufty Thomas and Juney Brown Toes ran away, disappearing into the deeper grass.

Colin had secured Falco, and they were soon at the spot where the Goshawk, Goose, struggled to take flight. Colin quieted it and secured it on his own, gloved hand.

'That's your turn done I think, Colin,' Liam said.

Chapter Three *Colin Sweevil*

Colin muttered angrily, but didn't reply. He moved from one Hawk to another, soothing them and making sure there was no more damage.

'It's your turn tonight, Yar,' Lord Snoot declared.

The Pharoahs Rob Auty

Chapter Four
Yar Turps

It was one o'clock in the morning, a very dark night indeed. Yar had two of his best dogs with him; Lurchers, called Biscuit and Barker. He'd insisted the other men stayed away, on the hill where they had stood when the Hawks had failed.

He moved silently, as in many hunts before; silence was a good ally. His dogs stayed at heel, both well-trained beasts.

Yar stopped and listened, annoyingly he could hear the other men yammering away in the distance, and so he moved away again, until that sound faded. Then he waited. Nearly an hour passed, and Yar did not move; he was a patient man. He was also very unsure on this night. He knew, sensed, the Hare would be in exactly the same place, waiting for him. Things were not as they should be, every instinct in the Hare should see her far, far away from here; therefore the Hare wasn't of natural origin. It was straightforward to Yar. He wanted the money; a chance to earn a thousand pounds was rare indeed.

He raised the heavy lamp he carried in his hand and pressed the *on* switch. A blinding, sun-bright, yellow beam scanned the area in front of him and he caught a brief glimpse of his prey before it ran.

Chapter Four *Yar Turps*

'On Biscuit, on Barker!' He shouted, his torch beam desperately trying to keep pace with the impossibly fast Hare.

Something landed on his head and he shouted in surprise, dropping the lamp and scrabbling at his face and head with both hands. Something above him squawked and pecked angrily at his hands. He screamed and grabbed for the lamp, swinging it wildly. Pointing it above him, he caught a brief flash of black and white feathers, and then he became aware of his dogs barking wildly.

He scanned ahead of himself with the powerful light and his heart skipped a beat. He dropped the lamp again in fear.

For a minute he did nothing, then he shouted, 'Away Biscuit, away Barker. Come on boys!' He picked up the lamp, and scanned it around again. Dozens of animals, Big Brown Rats, Rabbits, and Hares, ran hither and thither, teasing his frenzied dogs. 'Away dogs! Away!' Yar Turps, tinker and sometimes hunter, ran as if the Hounds of Hell chased him, the beam of light shaking crazily in the darkness in front of him.

Chapter Four *Yar Turps*

Interlude

'What's he doing, Mommy?' Patrick asked, puzzled.

'It's called *Lamping*, Patrick,' she told him. 'Hunters use a powerful beam to see the animals they're hunting at night. In some cases it startles the animals, freezing them, and in others it just reflects back off the eyes of the prey, allowing the hunters to shoot, or send their dogs.'

'Oh, not nice,' was all Patrick said in reply.

'Shall I continue?'

'Definitely!' said Patrick.

'That was dangerous, Mollie,' Juney admonished her feathered friend.

'Not really, I've wanted to peck more than one human in my time and it was very satisfying!' Mollie said.

The Golden Hare lay low in the long grass, Mollie perched on her head, and they watched the erratic beam of bright light bounce away, carried by the frightened man, his two yapping dogs following. All the other animals had already disappeared into the night.

'Yar, you are off your head, Old Man,' Liam stated calmly.

'Don't be an old fool, Yar,' Bograt added.

Chapter Four *Yar Turps*

'He might have a point,' Colin said uncomfortably, 'look at that Eagle yesterday.'

'I tell you there's magic afoot, that Hare stands her ground; other animals help her as well. I was attacked by a bloomin' Magpie, for goodness sake! In the middle of the night! Birds don't fly at night!' Yar was beside himself, and absently shone his still bright light in the other men's faces.

'No matter,' Lord Snoot declared, 'tomorrow, at noon, she'll have two dozen Hounds baying for her blood, and they'll run all day, and into the night if necessary!'

'No, not into the night! If you haven't got her by dark, then she's mine!' Liam said sternly.

'You're all stark staring mad. That Hare is dangerous, you'd be well to call the whole thing off before somethin' really bad happens,' Yar snapped. He switched off his lamp, got into his old Landrover with his dogs, and drove away.

The Pharoahs   *Rob Auty*

Chapter Five
Lord Snoot

Snoot sat astride a big bay horse, comfortable and lord-like. He was obviously at home on the beast.

They were back on the hill, staring across the space between themselves and the strange Hare. It was about noon, and the sun shone brightly above them, although clouds rumbled across the sky on the horizon, threatening rain later.

Liam was mounted on a

stallion that stood beside Snoot's horse. He was confident, and the horse was calm.

There were many more people here now. Dog handlers and stable hands from the Lord's estate. At least fifteen vehicles were parked to the rear in a makeshift car park.

'Do you ride?' Liam asked Colin, who was standing fearfully beside a gentle mare.

'No, not really,' Colin answered nervously.

Just then Bograt drove up on a large quad bike, and parked it beside the horses. 'You got room for a passenger on that?' Colin asked.

'Aye go on then,' Bograt said begrudgingly.

A relieved Colin got on the bike behind Bograt.

'Are we all ready then?' Snoot shouted.

His hounds took up the cry, howling and barking in excitement. More than twenty Beagles and five Harriers thundered down the hill towards the Hare.

'Tally Ho!' cried Snoot. He urged his horse after the Hounds.

Chapter Five   *Lord Snoot*

'Oh please!' Liam said dryly, but he turned his horse to pursue Snoot.

'Tally Ho,' Colin said, rather limply, from behind Bograt, who ignored his passenger and steered his quad bike over the bumpy ground, following the hunt.

'Are you ready for this, Juney?' Mollie asked, as she hovered above the Golden Hare.

'Yes, this is what I was made for, Mollie, they cannot catch me. Has everyone gone? Including Tufty?' she asked.

'Yes,' Mollie said, 'As you said, everyone is hidden or has fled the area. There will be no other scents, only yours, Juney.'

'Good', Juney said.

The baying Hounds were within a hundred yards. 'Time to run!' Juney said, and she took off, running impossibly fast, soon leaving the chasing Hounds far behind.

Juney Brown Toes, The Golden Hare, led both men and Hounds a merry chase. Beagles and their like can run and run and run. They, with other cousins, were bred to hunt Hare, relentlessly and without mercy.

Chapter Five *Lord Snoot*

But Juney was their master. Four hours into the hunt the Harrier Hounds gave up, falling back, and barking miserably at their tougher cousins.

Still Juney stayed well ahead, occasionally dropping back to ensure they did not lose her scent. At first she ran free, over fields and meadows, but as the sun began to dip in the western sky, she altered her path, and chose a rougher and tougher route. Through every hedge and wall she knew, she led them, struggling over fences and through abandoned byres.

About an hour after the Harriers gave up, Bograt, with Colin behind him, called it a day and headed back to the cars.

An exhausted Snoot soon followed, with Liam in tow, a wide grin across the big man's face.

The Beagles were nowhere to be seen, but both men could hear their soulful, sad baying, and it was coming closer as they neared the cars and other vehicles.

Remarkably the Golden Hare passed right by the startled Snoot and Liam, and the Hounds followed, upsetting the horses. Snoot fell to the ground with a bump and a squeal. Liam stayed in the saddle and brutally brought his horse under control.

The Hare bounded between the vehicles, the Hounds chased, and mayhem followed. Men and dogs struggled, shouted and barked, and through it all, the apparently mischievous Hare dodged and teased man and Hound mercilessly.

Chapter Five   *Lord Snoot*

Liam watched for a moment, until he saw what he wanted. The Hare was being corralled and moved slowly towards him. He quickly jumped from his horse and ran towards a rusty Landrover, skulking down next to a front wheel, out of sight of everyone.

Sure enough the Hare sped by. Liam dived. He was almost too slow, but he managed to grab a fistful of fur on the hind leg of the Hare. It squealed and kicked violently backwards, loosening the man's grip, and disappeared into the deepening darkness.

Liam got to his feet as the Hounds ran around his feet; they had given up the chase and were keen on something Liam held in his hand.

'Damn that Hare!' Snoot screeched as he approached the big man, and then he added, 'What have you got there, Liam?'

Bograt and Colin approached and the dog handlers hurriedly got the Hounds under control.

Liam didn't answer Snoot immediately; rather he walked over to his own, very expensive, four-wheel-drive vehicle and opened the large back door.

In the brightness provided by the car's interior lights Liam lifted his hand. 'Essence of The Golden Hare, Snoot.' He smiled and held his hand out for the Lord to see. He had a handful of golden hairs. 'My winning ticket, Lads,' he said arrogantly to anyone who cared to listen.

He turned and pushed his hand into the shadows of the boot. 'Cleopatra,' he cooed.

A sharp-faced, keen-eyed Hound lifted her head from amongst the other dogs in the car. 'I have something for you, Cleo, my Darling,' Liam let the Hound sniff his closed fist. The dog became very excited and alert. 'Good, Cleo, good,' Liam whispered. He then placed his arm deeper into the dark interior of the car and all those watching heard the excited yapping and barking.

Chapter Five Lord Snoot

Then Liam opened the lower part of the back door of the car and eight medium sized Hounds scrabbled from the vehicle.

'Meet my Hounds, Gentlemen,' Liam said, 'my Klieb tal-Fenek, my *Pharoahs*.'

Rameses

Interlude

'Klib … kleb?' Patrick asked, frowning.

'Klieb tal-Fenek. It's Maltese for Rabbit, or Hare Dogs. They're beautiful dogs, although apparently if you keep them as pets, you'd better not have a cat, or chickens, or any small pets,' Sam told him.

'I thought Maltese were chocolates?' Patrick asked innocently, although Samantha could see the cheeky glint in his eyes.

Chapter Five Lord Snoot

'You can do your homework if you want, it sounds like your geography needs some work.' Sam started to get up.

'No, read on, please!'

Samantha laughed, and then continued reading.

Juney ran until darkness stopped her, and the uncomfortable feeling of man's cruel hand had left her. 'That was close,' Mollie Magpie said, landing close to her friend.

'It was scary,' admitted Juney.

'You better be ready again soon, Juney. I think that man with the fiery hair is next, and I don't like the look of his dogs. I've never seen their like before. Smaller than Grey Hound, and their coats are the colour of the sunset!' Mollie settled on the side of the Golden Hare, who lay full length, allowing the ground to cool her.

'His touch felt cruel, almost evil, even Gryja didn't feel like that. Gryja is what he is, Spirit of the Wood and Hunt, but this flame-haired man feels bad, and he scares me, and so do his dogs.' The Golden Hare shuddered.

'No waiting on the hill this time, Juney, hide and make them find you. And if things go bad, look for Digger the Badger in Low Wood; he has promised to help The Golden Hare.'

Chapter Five *Lord Snoot*

The Pharoahs — Rob Auty

Chapter Six
Liam, and the Pharoahs

'Let's all have a cup of tea and some cake first,' Lord Snoot suggested. He looked tired and dejected. Most of his staff had left with the horses and Hounds. Just one retainer remained; he stood in the background, a flask and a biscuit box held dutifully in his hands.

Liam

Liam busied himself at his car, ushering eight of the Pharoah Hounds from the back of the vehicle. He paired them off and they obediently stood where he told them. He looked up and snorted a derisive laugh at Snoot. 'What? And let her get far away? I don't think so.'

Colin and Bograt joined the men. 'Nice looking Hounds, Liam,' Colin said.

'Thanks, Man. They are ancient hunting Hounds, originating from Malta. I'm going to use an old hunting technique tonight,' he told the others.

'I see you got your shotgun.' Yar Turps appeared out of the darkness.

'What of it, Turps? I thought you'd had enough humiliation for one day? Coming back for more?' Liam snarled.

'Just gonna tag along, make sure everything is fair like, if you know what I mean,' said Yar. He pulled back his long coat, revealing his own battered shotgun.

'You threatening me, Old Man?' Liam bristled, holding his own gun all the tighter.

'Not at all, not at all,' Yar gave them all a broken toothed grin.

'Tell us how you're going to use the dogs, Liam,' Colin interjected, trying to calm both men.

Liam gave Yar a final, hard look and then spoke again, 'I've been training them hard. This is a perfect test. I'll release the Hounds to the four compass points. One male and one female, they'll hunt the Hare using scent, and when one Hound catches the scent, the female will give chase and the dog will follow, making sure the quarry doesn't veer too far off. Their barks will bring the other Hounds, and us, and we'll chase that Golden Hare to ground!'

'And what then, Hares don't normally run to ground and if she does, do we use spades? Dig her out?' Snoot asked.

Wordlessly Liam pulled three spades from the boot, and gave them to a grumbling Bograt. Then he pulled a medium sized cage from the back of his vehicle, in it were three big Ferrets. 'These girls will get her out, and Cleopatra,' he stroked the head of one of his Hounds, 'can hear a Ferret three metres down, under the ground, and will know where our Hare is going to surface. Then we'll net her, and the bargaining can begin,' he said smugly.

'Just remember, that's my Hare!' Bograt shouted.

'I'll give you double anything he offers!' Snoot declared, looking angrily at Bograt.

'Double of nothin' is still nothin',' Yar told them. 'I'll be following.' Then he wandered off into the darkness.

'Stupid tinker!' Liam shouted at the shadows.

Chapter Six *Liam, and The Pharoahs*

Juney hid herself in the gully, behind the farm, where the little girl and Farmer lived. She felt some comfort there. The red-haired man frightened her, and she hadn't been frightened since she had become The Golden Hare. She knew she could outrun the man, and was fairly confident about the mysterious dogs. But she was unsettled and her confidence waned. She hunkered down, chewed absently on some dried grass and then tried to sleep.

'Away, Cleopatra, away Rameses!' Liam excitedly urged the Hounds to run. He carried a big torch and had given similar tools to the other men. Cleo and Rameses were the last pair of dogs to be released.

'What now?' Snoot asked. He was cold and uncomfortable, and wanted to be at home in front of a large fire, with a large brandy.

'We'll follow Cleo. I fancy she'll be the one to catch the scent first,' Liam answered.

The men trudged along behind Liam, their torch beams bouncing before them.

It wasn't long before they heard an excited barking in the distance, accompanied by many more from all directions. 'Told you! She's got the scent! That Hare is mine, come on!' Liam ran ahead. The others followed more slowly and if they'd been observant they would have noticed a man in a heavy coat walking a parallel path just out of the torchlight.

Juney trembled in excitement and fear. She waited until she saw the shadow of the fast moving Hound enter the cut and then she ran. She was soon well ahead of her pursuer and was feeling easier, when something barged into her. She realised it was another dog and she rolled away, out of reach of the snapping jaws.

Chapter Six *Liam, and The Pharoahs*

She was up again in an instant and running. She sensed, rather than saw, several other Hounds around her, driving her one way. She jinked, changed direction, and nearly ran into yet another dog, dodging its dive towards her and running into the farmyard she knew so well. Here she gained some distance and really opened up, running up the moonlit Black Death Road.

The Pharoahs followed, ever closer.

'There! Up the road, the Hare!' Liam shouted and without thinking he raised his shotgun and fired. The other men shouted their anger. Yar Turps stepped once more out of the shadows and placed himself between Liam and The Golden Hare.

Interlude

'They said no guns!' An indignant Patrick jumped up from the couch. 'I don't like Liam!'

'Shall I stop, Patrick?' Samantha asked gently.

'No way! Liam better get his though!' he answered.

'Let's find out shall we?'

'Yes!'

Chapter Six *Liam, and The Pharoahs*

Juney squealed as a hot, sharp pain hit her in the rear legs. She didn't know it, but two pellets from Liam's shotgun blast had hit her; shotguns fire a single shell, full of tiny pellets, which spread out as they leave the barrel of the gun, making it a sometimes indiscriminate weapon.

The Golden Hare staggered but then kept running. At first she was fine but soon she felt the effects of the pellets and slowed down. She heard the Hounds closing and so she turned sharply left, through a Hare-size hole in the wall, and ran blindly across the outer farm fields and into Low Wood, home of the Badgers. The sky above cleared rapidly and a full moon gave her pursuers what they needed.

The Pharoahs, all eight of them, scrabbled over the wall and followed The Golden Hare into the wood.

'Get out of my way!' Liam shone his torch into Yar's face.

Yar shaded his eyes with one hand and raised his shotgun with the other. 'We said no guns, Liam,' he told the big man.

'That's right!' Colin shouted.

'If you shoot her with that blunderbuss I won't give you a penny for the pelt,' Snoot declared, waving his torch indignantly.

'Alright, alright,' Liam said, 'I won't fire again, it was just instinct. Besides my Hounds will have her soon. Listen to that, let's go!'

They all heard the excited barking of Liam's Pharoahs.

The light from the torches fell on the Hounds. They milled excitedly around a hole in the side of a tree-lined banking.

Chapter Six *Liam, and The Pharoahs*

Colin had been carrying the Ferret cage for Liam, and he handed it to the red-haired man. 'I wouldn't, Liam,' Yar said.

'What are you talking about, Tinker?' Liam asked as he picked two Ferrets from the cage.

'Badgers. This here's a Badger sett. It wouldn't be a good idea,' Yar suggested again. Yar wasn't really worried; he just didn't want to see the Ferrets hurt. It was a surprising change in his character, particularly to Yar himself; soon after his failure Lamping the Hare, he'd had an inordinate desire to help it and all the animals.

'Get lost, Old Man,' Liam hissed, and then he pushed the Ferrets into the hole.

Juney sat in the darkness, and vainly waited for her eyes to adjust. Hares have pretty good night vision, but here in the depths of the Badger sett there was very little she was able to make out. Rather she let her other senses do the work, and her nose and ears twitched furiously.

'You are safe here, Golden Hare,' Meles said, as he sat beside the Hare.

'Thank you, Meles, you've saved me. My legs are very sore,' Juney told him.

Digger was closer to the surface than Juney and Meles. He stood with younger Badgers and confronted the Ferrets. 'You want something, Cousins?' he asked the smaller, wiry animals. The Ferrets stopped, looked at each other, and then they turned and ran for the entrance of the burrow, without looking back.

Chapter Six   *Liam, and The Pharoahs*

Liam danced an involuntary dance as the Ferrets ran around his feet. 'What the…'

'Oh dear,' Yar laughed.

Liam furiously picked up the Ferrets and placed them back in the cage. He took a spade off Bograt, and began to furiously dig at the bank. After a minute he turned, 'Well?' He looked at Bograt, Colin and Snoot in turn.

Bograt grudgingly joined him, and then Colin. Snoot shrugged and rubbed his back. 'I'll hold the torches,' he offered with a smile.

Liam shook his head angrily and then turned to continue digging.

Badgers are secretive, timid creatures normally. But Digger was a bit different. For a start he was very big for a Badger, which sometimes gave him a false sense of power ... well perhaps not. Badgers *are* strong, with powerful front claws for digging, and a strange jaw, which can only move from side to side, and up and down, able to bite down with a fearful force; their hides are tough, and they have a thick layer of fat, that can act as added protection; they also have an uncanny knack of practically twisting inside their skins. They aren't normally aggressive, but Digger, as I said, was different...

Digger the Badger

The men had stepped back from the hole, and Ramases and the other dogs, except for Cleopatra, dived into the newly dug hole and began their own excitable excavation. A black and white hurricane burst from the hole and set about the Hounds. The dogs barked furiously and attacked their assailant.

Ramases squealed as Digger got a vice-like grip on one of his front legs. The Badger had to let go though, as he was attacked by the other four Hounds. Liam screamed his anger and tried to level his shotgun but Yar grabbed the barrel. 'We said NO GUNS,' Yar shouted forcefully. Colin and Bograt were backing off, and Snoot turned and ran away.

Digger bit more of the Hounds, and they bit him, but their bites had little effect on the thick hide of the Badger.

Liam dragged his gun from Yar's grasp and pointed it at the tinker. 'I'll shoot you if you do anything like that again,' he shouted above the din of the barking and furious growling.

Chapter Six — Liam, and The Pharoahs

Interlude

'Go, Digger!' Patrick shouted excitedly. 'I like Badgers!'

'I'll read on shall I?' Samantha asked patiently.

'Yes!' Patrick said, sitting back down.

'I'll have to go, Juney. Turn and follow this tunnel, stay straight and you will come out deeper in Low Wood,' Meles told her; then he turned and headed towards the commotion nearer the surface. Juney did as she was told and struggled down the tunnel. Moving steadily upwards, she saw a lighter patch in the blackness ahead of her and headed towards it.

The Hounds bayed and barked and attacked the Badger, and Liam struggled to get a beam of light on it, let alone bring his shotgun to bear.

Then a dozen other Badgers appeared, moving into and out of the torch beams; and then more. The Pharoahs lost heart at this latest turn of events and ran off, Ramases limping after them.

Chapter Six *Liam, and The Pharoahs*

Liam ran after his dogs, and the Badgers disappeared below ground once again.

'Well that was interesting, and I can't help feeling a little smug, I got a lot closer to catching a Hare than anyone else,' Colin said agreeably.

'Aye, ya did, Colin, and the Badgers were interesting alright,' Yar agreed, 'No Golden Hare for you, Bograt,' he added.

'I don't care, I'm tired, and cold, and I'm going home,' Bograt declared miserably.

'I'll go with you,' Colin said.

'I'll stick around; I like the dark of the woods, lots to see in the moonlight.' Yar smiled at the men, 'Good evenin' gents.'

None of them noticed the excited Pharoah, Cleopatra. She had caught a scent again, and ran into the deep dark behind the Badger sett.

The Pharoahs — *Rob Auty*

Cleo

Chapter Seven
Help from the Darkness

Juney moved as fast as she could. Her rear legs hurt terribly and she was tired. She had been too brave, she chided herself, but she had won, defeating all the hunters. Then behind her, she heard a rustle and a low, excited growl.

She broke into a stuttering run and entered a small moonlit clearing, and behind her a Pharoah Hound followed.

'I will eat you, Hare,' the Hound said, through barks and growls.

Juney tried to run but couldn't. Instead she dragged herself, as quickly as she could, under a thorny bush. The Pharoah snapped at her feet and Juney pulled her body into a tight ball. The Hound grew frantic, digging and biting at the bush, tearing it apart, leaving The Golden Hare exposed.

And then a deep, deep growl sounded from the clearing, and Cleopatra was turned, startled from her ravings, by the power in the sound.

Juney lifted her head, and watched the quivering Hound; it was frozen in terror for a moment, and then, at the sound of an even deeper growl, the Pharoah ran from the clearing, yelping like a puppy.

Whatever creature was the source of the growl, Juney knew, was sure to be the end of her. But she decided to face it on her feet and she scrambled from her hiding place to see the shimmering shape of a Wolf.

Chapter Seven *Help from the Darkness*

'Golden Hare,' the Wolf said.

'Gryja?' Juney asked incredulously.

'You are mine, Golden Hare; my hunt, my prey, my challenge. I will not sit by and watch a skinny whelp of a Hound drag you from a bush and kill you while you are injured. Had she caught you on a proper hunt, then I would not have interfered,' Gryja's words answered her unasked questions.

'Thank you ... I think,' Juney said.

'You are welcome, Golden Hare. Until next we meet.' Gryja's shade disappeared.

Chapter Eight
Yar Turps and Samantha

Juney didn't remember much of the rest of the night. She struggled back to Black Death Road and moved slowly to the farm. She had a vague idea of what she was doing, but she passed out in the farmyard.

Samantha was home alone, something that didn't happen often, but Farmer had gone out, promising not to be too long, and her mother was away, at school, watching her brother in a play. She looked out the front window absently, and then took a frantic closer look, before swinging open the front door and running out. 'Beauty! What happened?' Sam knelt beside the stricken Hare and gently stroked The Golden Hare's side.

Sam wasn't sure what to do, but she picked Juney up and cradled her still form. 'You are cold,' Sam said, taking the Hare back into the house and picking up a thick towel in the kitchen to wrap the Hare in.

Sam looked at the clock and made a decision; she would walk up Farm Road, towards the village, and hopefully meet her father coming home. It was clear the Hare needed help, and Tim, the vet, was the man to give that help. He had an office in the village.

Chapter Eight   *Yarp Turps and Samantha*

She struggled to lock the door, and then was on her way. She'd only gone a few yards when a Magpie landed on the road in front of her. The bird looked at her with one black eye, and Sam instinctively knew what she should do. 'I'm taking her to the vet in the village,' she told the Magpie. Remarkably the bird nodded enthusiastically at her, and Sam continued on.

Only a moment later an old Landrover pulled up beside her, and Yar Turps got out. 'What you got there, Sam?' he asked.

Sam liked Yar; he was a good friend of her father. 'I found her, in the farmyard,' she told him, opening her arms a little to show Yar the Hare.

'Right! Get in the 'Rover now, Missie,' Yar told her, as he opened the door for her. 'Men are hunting her, and it wouldn't be safe for her if they found you.'

'Hunting her! Hunting Beauty? Who?' Sam asked indignantly.

'Bograt, Snoot, and Liam,' he said. 'Come on, Miss, in the car!'

Samantha carefully climbed into the front passenger seat of the Landrover, being very gentle with Juney. Yar got in the other side and started the engine. They set off at a brisk pace, the Landrover chugging along.

Sam was amazed to see the Magpie flying alongside of them. She'd seen one or two odd things where Beauty was concerned, but this one still made her eyes widen considerably. The car was in the village in five minutes, and two or three more minutes negotiating traffic found them parked a short walk from the vet's office. Samantha got out of the Landrover and headed straight towards the vet's surgery.

Chapter Nine
Tim the 'Vet-n-ary'

'That's done, Liam,' Tim, the veterinarian, said nervously to a grim looking Liam.

'Just as well, Ramases was a good dog, but useless to me lame,' Liam replied with a shrug.

'It was a shame, Liam, he was a young dog.'

'Aye, well, my choice, not yours, Tim; put it on my account.' And with that the big man left the treatment room.

Tim sighed, putting down a healthy animal was not to his liking, and Liam was not to his liking either. The red-haired man treated his animals badly, and Tim often toyed with the idea of refusing to serve him, but Tim wouldn't do that, he would worry too much about the big man's dogs.

Loud shouting brought him out of his reverie. Something was going on in the waiting room. He walked quickly through a short corridor and found Liam towering over little Samantha and shouting at her. Yar Turps, the tinker, was there as well, and he was struggling to hold Liam back.

'Stop it, Liam!' Tim could be assertive when he chose, and the men stopped arguing. Tim approached Samantha, she looked scared, and he asked her, 'What have you got there, Sam?'

Sam stepped away from Liam and opened her arms saying, 'This is Beauty. She's a Hare and she's been hurt.'

Chapter Nine	Tim the 'Vet-n-ary'

'Forget it, Tim. That is mine!' Liam pointed at the Hare.

Tim ignored him and carefully examined the Hare in Sam's arms.

'Stop bein' a bully, Liam,' Yar said.

'Get lost, Tinker, before I lose my temper,' Liam growled menacingly.

'Both of you, out! Get out of my surgery now or I'll call the constable! Out!' Tim pointed to the door until the men had left. Liam looked back and his face said plainly he'd be back.

'Bring her in here, Sam.' Tim turned and led Samantha to the treatment room. 'Right put her down on the table, Sam.'

'Is she going to be alright?' Sam asked, her voice trembling slightly. Liam had clearly frightened her.

Tim busied himself for a minute and then looked up at Sam … and then past her. A Magpie sat on his filing cabinet.

Sam turned and looked at the bird and then said, 'Oh, that's Beauty's friend.'

'O … k…' Tim stammered, took another look at the Magpie, and then returned his attention to the examination of the Hare, which was regaining consciousness. 'She's been shot, but not badly so,' he told Samantha, 'just two pellets, though I think they're pretty deep, and her moving won't help.' He struggled to hold the Hare, who was fully awake now.

'Tell her he's going to make her better,' Sam told the Magpie.

Chapter Nine *Tim the 'Vet-n-ary'*

The bird hopped onto the table and twittered busily at the Hare, which stopped struggling, and went limp again.

Tim was dumbstruck; he couldn't believe what he was seeing. He recovered somewhat though, and in spite of his disbelief he spoke to the bird himself, 'Tell … her I need to put her to sleep for a while, so I can remove the pellets.'

Once again the Magpie twittered furiously, and the Hare actually nodded.

Tufty Thomas, Slow Freddy, Digger, and many other Hares and animals moved to the outskirts of the village.

'We have to rescue The Golden Hare!' Digger declared; he was bullish after his run-in with the Pharoahs.

'We will wait,' Slow Freddy said, 'we have a history with the little girl. She has helped the

Hares on more than one occasion, and Mollie is with Juney. We wait.'

Chapter Ten
Farmer

Tim took off his surgical mask and nodded to the nurse, who took the Hare to a nearby cage, so the

animal could sleep off the effects of the anaesthetic. Tim walked back to the reception area and sat down beside Sam. 'She will be fine, the pellets have not done too much damage, and she will make a full recovery,' he told her.

Sam replied with a hug. Tim pulled away a little self-consciously and stood up, just as the front door burst open. Liam, Lord Snoot, and Bograt, along with several unsavoury characters from the local pub came in.

'Get out!' Tim demanded.

'Give me the Hare, Tim. Now,' Liam said in a low threatening voice.

'It's ours!' Snoot added.

'It's cost me a lot of money!' Bograt screeched.

'It cost me a dog!' Liam said.

'You decided to put your dog down, Liam,' Tim said. 'The Hare didn't kill your dog, you did.'

'Actually a Badger helped,' Yar Turps said. He was just coming through the door, with Farmer, Samantha's dad, in tow.

'Tinker, you're really starting to annoy me now,' Liam hissed.

'Not half as much as you've annoyed me!' Farmer said; he grabbed Liam by the collar and, despite being

Chapter Ten *Farmer*

a smaller man, pulled Liam's head down, so the men were face to face. 'YOU DO NOT SHOUT AT MY DAUGHTER UNDER ANY CIRCUMSTANCES. DO YOU UNDERSTAND ME?' Farmer was furious, and Liam's knees buckled. Farmer, despite his size, was incredibly strong, and Liam could feel that strength. 'Now get out, ALL OF YOU!'

The men scrabbled over each other to leave, Liam first, pushing his way past the others.

'Well done,' Tim said to Farmer, 'I don't know what I would have done if you hadn't come along.'

'You'd ha done alright, Tim,' Yar said. 'Liam's a bully; I've seen him back down time and again when pressed. He's big and all that, but he's a small man really.'

Farmer hugged Samantha. 'Are you alright, Sam?' he asked.

'I'm fine and Beauty is fine,' she said, 'but how are we going to get her out of here? Those men want to kill her, I think!'

'Don't worry, Sam,' Tim said, 'this place is pretty secure all locked up, and they'll cool down after a couple of days.'

'And me n' your da' will take her somewhere secret to free her when she's ready,' Yar told her.

'And the hunters want to get her, but Farmer and the girl won't let them, and the vet-n-ary says he'll protect her too,' Mollie Magpie finished her breathless report to the rest of the animals.

'Right Mice and Rats into the village and keep a lookout on the vet-n-ary place; come tell us if the hunters do anything. The rest of us will wait, but if The Golden Hare is in danger we will act,' Slow Freddy declared. The other animals obeyed the newly confident Hare without question.

Several dozen Brown Rats, and fifty or so Field Mice raced away into the night.

Chapter Ten *Farmer*

The Pharoahs   Rob Auty

Chapter Eleven
The Animals, and
One Giant Rat

Juney lay on the soft blanket and watched the door to the cage. She felt safe, but couldn't help feeling unsettled, caged as she was. Her legs felt fine, she had two severe itches she couldn't reach, and they were keeping her awake. She wouldn't ever know but Tim had stitched her in the two places, with special stitches, which would dissolve in time.

It was night, Juney could see stars through a high window, and she yearned to be running free.

A bang and a shattering noise alerted her, and she moved to the back of the cage fearfully.

Liam fiddled with the lock on the Vet's office door. He'd smashed the window and now he opened the door. He rushed in and pressed the keypad on the wall deactivating the alarm, before it had time to sound. He'd seen Tim do it many times, and 1111 was a stupidly simple code. 'Simple,' he said to Bograt, who was the only one who would follow him on his dangerous scheme.

'Be quiet!' Bograt whispered nervously.

'Shut up, and follow me,' Liam said dismissively.

Chapter Eleven *The Animals, and One Giant Rat*

He knew where he was going.

The Rats had reported, and Slow Freddy had acted. Hundreds of animals, Badgers, Hares, Rabbits, Mice, even a Fox or two, and many others followed the burglars into the surgery.

Liam reached the room he was looking for and opened the door; there she was, nicely caged for him. He grabbed the cage and turned. Bograt was standing; mouth agape, looking at something.

'I've got her, let's get out of here!' Liam said, a little too loudly.

'Lo … okkk!' Bograt gasped.

Liam moved towards the reception, pushing past Bograt. He stopped in his tracks and dropped the cage.

He screamed and tried to run forward, but a big Badger charged him.

Liam fell backwards and the Badger ran straight over him and finished face to face with the big man. Before he could get up dozens of the other beasts ran and covered him. He lay still, terrified.

Bograt huddled in a corner, snivelling in fear; a big Brown Rat stood upright in front of him, on guard.

Chapter Eleven *The Animals, and One Giant Rat*

Interlude

'Yeah!' Partick whooped. 'Liam's got it!'

'It appears so, but shall we read the rest, there's not much more to go?' Samantha asked.

'Ok!' Patrick said.

Tufty Thomas got to the farm and without hesitation, ran up to the door, turned around, and gave the door a mighty bang with his powerful back legs. Then he ran a few yards away and waited. A light came on above the door and Farmer peered out. Seeing Tufty Thomas didn't seem to surprise him too much. 'Right where to?' he asked the big Jack.

Farmer with Yar, who he'd called, walked into the vet's office, both carried shotguns. Yar put the lights on and both men stopped dead. 'As I live and breath,' Farmer gasped. Yar's eyes all but popped out of his head.

A Magpie chattered loudly and the animals started to file out of the office. Neither man moved as the menagerie marched past them. The big Badger was last to move. Bograt stayed where he was, muttering inanely to himself. Liam jumped up and shook himself vigorously, and then he picked up Juney's cage. 'Put it down, carefully,'

Chapter Eleven *The Animals, and One Giant Rat*

Farmer said, raising his shotgun.

Liam looked like he wanted to protest, but Farmer's eyes suggested he shouldn't.

'What's all this then?' the Constable said as he entered the office.

The Pharoahs   Rob Auty

Hare Epilogue

'Liam and Bograt got off with a warning and a fine,' Farmer said. He, Sam, and Yar walked through the cornfield, towards High Meadow.

Sam was carrying the cage with Beauty in. 'They should have gone to prison!' she said, indignantly.

'They kind o' have, Missie,' Yar said. 'They're both a laughing stock in the village and the pub, particularly Bograt, with his stories about a 'Giant Rat' and monster Badgers. Liam keeps his mouth shut, and ain't bigmouthed no more.'

They reached the wall and clambered over it, entering High Meadow. 'Here, Sam?' Farmer asked.

'Yes,' she replied, putting down the cage and opening its door.

Juney ran from the cage, fast as lightening, no ill effects from her injuries. And as she joyfully bounded around the meadow, it filled with animals, ready to greet The Golden Hare.

The people turned and began to climb the wall; Juney ran over to them, and with several other Hares, she banged her hind leg on the ground in gratitude, the only way she knew to convey her thanks.

The girl turned around, and The Golden Hare looked her in the eyes, and realised Samantha did understand.

A Hunter's Epilogue

Liam sat close to the fireplace in the pub, and stared into the flames. The door swung inwards and let cold air in. Liam lifted his head and smiled as a slovenly man, with a flat cap on his head, walked in. He'd been waiting for this man.

Bradey Smith was the best Badger man in the region.

Epilogue

'You can't end like that, does that mean Digger and Meles are in trouble?'

Patrick asked.

'You'll have to wait … until I finish writing it; it's one of the unfinished Tales,' Samantha told him.

'Oh, Mummy!'

'Go do your homework, so I can do mine,' she waved the Hare's Tales papers at Patrick.

Coming Soon

A Hare's Tale 4
Digger's Courage

www.ingramcontent.com/pod-product-compliance
Lightning Source LLC
Chambersburg PA
CBHW031125080526
44587CB00011B/1111